Ex Vivo
(Out of the Living Body)

Poems

Kirsten Casey

Hip Pocket Press Mission Statement

It is our belief that the arts are the embodiment of the soul of a culture, that the promotion of writers and artists is essential if our current culture, with its emphasis on television and provocative outcomes, is to have a chance to develop that inner voice and ear that express and listen to beauty. Toward that end, Hip Pocket Press will continue to search out and discover poets and writers whose voices can give us a clearer understanding of ourselves and of the culture which defines us.

Other Books from Hip Pocket Press

You Notice the Body: Gail Rudd Entrekin (poetry)
Terrain: Dan Bellm, Molly Fisk, Forrest Hamer (poetry)
A Common Ancestor: Marilee Richards (poetry)
Sierra Songs & Descants: Poetry & Prose of the Sierra
Truth Be Told: Tom Farber (epigrams)
Songs for a Teenage Nomad: Kim Culbertson (young adult fiction)
Yuba Flows: Kirsten Casey, Gary Cooke, Cheryl Dumesnil, Judy Halebsky, Iven Lourie & Scott Young (poetry)
The More Difficult Beauty: Molly Fisk (poetry)

Web Publications

Canary, a Literary Journal of the Environmental Crisis:
    hippocketpress.org/canary
Sisyphus, Essays on Language, Culture & the Arts:
    hippocketpress.org/sisyphus

Ex Vivo
(Out of the Living Body)

Kirsten Casey

Orinda, CA
2012

Published by Hip Pocket Press
5 Del Mar Court
Orinda, CA 94563
www.hippocketpress.org

This edition was produced for on-demand distribution by lightningsource.com for Hip Pocket Press.

Typesetting: Wordsworth (wordsworthofmarin.com)
Cover art: Kirsten Casey
Cover design: Brook Design Group (brookdesign.com)
Author photo: Hannah Casey
Proofreading assistance: Judy Crowe

Copyright 2012 by Kirsten Casey

No part of this book may be reproduced or transmitted in any form or by any means, graphic, electronic or mechanical, including photocopying, recording, taping or by any information storage or retrieval system, without permission in writing from the publisher.

Printed in the United States of America.

ISBN: 0-917658-37-X
978-0-917658-37-2

For Mark: You get me.

ACKNOWLEDGMENTS

Some of these poems first appeared in:

Santa Clara Review: "Full Term." *Canary*: "Learning About Trees." *Yuba Flows* (Hip Pocket Press, December 2008): "Bad Girl," "Maxine Remembers the Goats," "1976 Gonzales, California," "J.M. Barrie," "Painless," "A question that you should say yes to," "Take it back," "Falling Senseless," "Reunion of the Separated," "An Inebriated Monk Illuminating a Great Text," "In a Goddamn Hotel Room," "The Right Way to Say Goodbye," "Obituary for a New York Corpse."

Some of the poems in this collection were also part of a manuscript, *The First Piece of Everything Else,* which was a semi-finalist for the Pablo Neruda Poetry Prize in 2008.

THANKS

Thanks and love to my parents, Tom and Gwen Gorman, who gave me a happy childhood, filled with the constant presence of music, art, and humor. Thank you for giving me two beautiful sisters, Mary and Katie, whom I love dearly. There is no laughter like sister laughter. Thank you for (among many other things): making all of those school lunches, letting me stay up to watch "Saturday Night Live," tolerating my road-trip vomiting syndrome, putting me through college, and not freaking out when I majored in English.

To my three children, Nick, Hannah, and Ellie, who aren't that into poetry but have made my poetry better. Thank you for being three very different children. You know how to keep it interesting, and I love you. Also, thank you for laughing at my jokes.

To the family I married into: the Caseys, Gianottis and Frasers. Thank you for sharing over twenty years of babies, birthday marches, sporting events, family dinners, weddings, and fabulous stories (that change just a little in every retelling.) Don't worry, I will give you new names in my novel. I love you all.

Thank you to my writing group: Kim Culbertson, Ann Keeling, Jaime Williams, and Alicia Vandevorst. We are a force of chatter and similes. Without our meetings, this book would never have come to fruition. In particular, Kim, thank you for asking a complete stranger to join your group seven years ago. Friend, I owe you, forever.

To Gail and Charles Entrekin for their support of my work, for their personal bravery, and for their spectacular talent. I am in awe of both of you. Thank you, always.

To the fabulous women who generously agreed to write blurbs on this book: Molly Fisk, Cheryl Dusmenil, and Judy Halebsky. You are gifted poets, with extraordinary individual voices. I am grateful to you, and I am honored by your kindness.

NOTES:

"A question that you should say yes to" is a lyric from the song "Question" by Rhett Miller.

"Twister" is for Tracey Presslor, Will Norton's aunt.

The medical condition illustrated in "Painless" is Congenital Insensitivity to Pain with Anhidrosis, or CIPA.

The medical condition narrated in "The Ability to Forget" is hyperthymesia, also known as superior autobiographical memory.

Patrice de La Tour du Pin (1911-1975) was a French Catholic poet who was imprisoned in Germany during World War II. He wrote *Une somme de poesie*, which is a three-part work about man's relationship to himself; his relation to the world; and a relationship in which poetry becomes a form of prayer.

Eugene O'Neill's last words were: "I knew it. I knew it. Born in a hotel room, and goddamn it, died in a hotel room."

The sea wasp is a species of box jellyfish (*Chironex fleckeri*), and one of the most venomous creatures in the world.

CONTENTS

Intus Foras

Ex Vivo   15
Coincidence   17
Fencing   18
Melody   19
My dearest Theo,   21
Why I wasn't considered   22
meat and mineral   23
Obituary for a New York Corpse   24
Deprivation Litany   25
The things that don't happen   26
The poem I did not write   27
Goodbye to paper   28
Reunion of the Separated   30
Slain American as a Piece of Paper   32
The thing I like best about you   33
Autopsy Portrait   34
Lies   36
Painless   37
Sound   38
Falling Senseless   39
My four favorite bones   40
Thought upon Waking   41
The Suspicious Grieving   42
Broken   44
Where will they find the pieces?   46

Ex Vivo

For my husband, misdiagnosed with a malignant tumor   49
The Suicide Poem   50
I have no right to grieve you   51
What do you choose?   52
A question that you should say yes to   53
1976 Gonzales, California   54
Bad Girl   55
An inebriated monk illuminating a great text   56
The cellist's lament   57
Turbulence   58
Twister   60
Middle Name   61
Learning About Trees   62
In a Goddamn Hotel Room   64
Take it back,   66
Yosemite Fall   68
J.M. Barrie   69
Honeymoon   70
The right way to say goodbye   72
What we wear in the snow   74
Maxine remembers the goats   75
The ability to forget   76
I am not kissing you   78
The Narrator   80
Waiting for a sign   82
The important poem   83
Witness   84

Versions of myself 86
Praying Mantis 87
Keyhole 88
Sea Wasp 89
Patrice de la Tour du Pin 90
Love writes a letter 91
Thirty Days 92
Full Term 93
What do you think about me being sad? 95

What we feel and think and are is to a great extent
   determined by the state of our ductless glands and viscera.
                              Aldous Huxley

You don't have a soul. You are a soul. You have a body.
                              C.S. Lewis

And your very flesh shall be a great poem.
                              Walt Whitman

Intus Foras

Ex Vivo

(outside the living body; denoting removal of an organ for
reparative surgery, after which it is returned to the original site)

Our words uncoil like 28 feet of intestines,
specific and glistening on a stainless steel stretcher,
inside out, but still doing their job.
This angled and loopy tangle, in the dialect of the body,
is what we keep hidden in patterns, and what we
allow to leak out, warm and streaming.
We may be gutted, but we are still connected,
pulsing. And somehow, we are both the surgeon
and the patient. What we need to fix
is taken out under the brightest lights,
examined and rearranged under the limits
of time. We can last only so long outside
of ourselves, completely opened, vulnerable
to what might infect us the deepest,
to what might be too damaged, irreparable.

Every word is a vital organ.
What needs to be said cannot be replaced
by other things that need to be said.

But what comes out of the living body
can be returned to it. All of our parts
are desperate to revisit their proper place
in the order of things, to belong again
to where they came from.

This homecoming of words, this quiet return
to sequence and sentence, requires the scalpel's red seam,
a blood ringed opening, hours of tedious mending,
and the artistry of stitching pieces together again.
What keeps us alive is a potential for reorder,
this reinvention of everything inside of us.
Doctor and poet, go ahead;
what we take out, we are allowed
to put back in again.

Coincidence

Every boy I ever loved
has carried a pocket knife,
a blade on a ring, in a palm,
hanging low in a front denim pocket.

An innocent pippin apple sliced crossways
reveals a seeded star. The bark of a cedar tree, gouged
with love's alphabet, initials like burled knots, becomes
sawdust graffiti. Package twine pulled tight and cut
curls like tiny snakes on the floor.

Does it mean I longed for the reliable?
Was it that I saved time, never needing
scissors? Or was it simply the lure
of a real weapon, and the near danger
that comes with honed steel, hidden,
but so easily opened, with sharp purpose?

Fencing

Instead of hammering planks, the wood grain aligned,
the boards nailed, we slice
the air between us with swords.
That cage on your face, like mother's colander
used to strain blueberries
for Sunday muffins. We dress all
in white, as if for baptism, to see the blood leak
if a tip slips through skin.
The uniform does not flatter, the tops
snap like a baby suit, between our legs.
The safety pads and guards make us look irregular,
and creased, unlike the smooth ballerinas
in their satin slimness. We grip silver handles,
miniature tin umbrellas turned upside down. Our blades
bend and sing, from contact, from force, from resisting
the oxygen between us, swinging loopy Os
and Cs. And as much as you don't want to,
you want to cut something into me. Something
to mark your skill. Something raised and permanent,
like relief patterns carved on a granite headstone,
or a too-familiar voice choosing words
that pierce cotton and metal. I hold a defensive stance,
knees slightly bent, and although my weapon
is ready and raised, both of my arms are open.

Melody

A crooked staircase of blackened notes
climbs the page.
The lopsided clothesline stretches taut
between two poles, dots blow and spin
in summer's late afternoon breeze.
Shadowed faces of prisoners press up against
the sideways bars of treble and bass.
Each note is assigned an alphabetical letter,
a language beginning at middle C, the epicenter,
and aftershocks on hidden strings
decide tune and tempo.

Shouldn't complex chords and harmonic phrases
be named for colors rather than letters?
The more sharps—the truer the red,
the sound of fresh blisters, tiny stab wounds that
dissect ledger lines. Like fish sinking
the flats are always falling
into gray, a deep shimmer
of still scale and open eyes
trailing a clear line that twists
in the depths.

Why is it we are drawn to certain melodies?
We connect like the link-and-coupling pin
between railroad cars, locked into place,
with no choice but to follow the tracks
and watch through smudged glass the distance
covered, the blur of midnight tree trunks
and the moonlight between them, like piano keys.

The place in the brain, pale and finger-shaped,
curls an invitation, asks us over. Little triggers
in a series of notes hit nerve cells with the force
of grenades, each detonation reminding
we are designed to feel music; just as toddlers mimic
the words *no* and *hot* and *up*, this other language
is already a sense. We surrender to the repetitive chorus;
we feel the compulsion to lift the needle arm and return
it to the wide, beginning groove again and again.
These patterns of firings are not the executioner's
machine gun, are not the loud shot of an aging engine.
We are on a plaid blanket beneath the invisible fireworks
of our brains' black sky.

The composer and poet, distant first cousins,
sit and stare at a white page, already a flat ghost of
possibility, blank, but already an elegy. To write, both need
a paned wooden window to distract and inspire, both want
smudges of pencil and a particular indigo ink.
The walls between them, the streets, the measured miles,
the moment between now and the first line drawn,
separate them. Every poet writes a song
that has no melody, and every word secretly wants
to be a lyric. Even now, the poet sits alone, wondering
how much more would my poem be if it had a tune?

My dearest Theo,

Tonight St. Remy paints itself.
I see markings in the clouds,
the wind trails scratch marks in swirls.
Stars spin and tumble
like bright children rolling down
a hillside. The air is thick and slow
like breathing glue. Each rooftop pierces
the sky—cuts without blood, every shade
of purple in a bruise.
I've run out of blue paint,
and it seems the only pigment
beyond this window is blue—
from steeple shadow to the low bellies
of thunderheads, to the deep-thatched rows
in the vineyards.
I want to drag my brush
through the sky, steal sticky stars
for this canvas, now awash
with last strokes of indigo. I want
to swallow this night like a true, black elixir,
a whole ripe plum, or my own tongue.
The bottles you sent by post are empty brown,
the color of dead stems. I poured them
into the base of my hydrangea, now grown
wild, without bloom.

Ever yours,
Vincent

Why I wasn't considered

Perhaps it was the lisp,
or not so much the lisp, but my constant
apologizing for it. The exhausting
sound of sorry. My speaking
has always made me smaller, turned
my shoulders in, as if playing
charades, I am a whisper.
But then again, they may not have
considered me at all, not the smirk
disguised as a smile, not my propensity
for sweat stains, or inclination to answer
questions with the word *Indeed*.
What I would beg you to consider,
my page acquaintance, please take
a moment's time to recognize
that the simple order of my words
becomes me.

meat and mineral

the bloody butcher's apron
repeated patterns of damp hands
wrung on white cotton
a mini crime scene

he studied the broken lines
dividing the rump and loin
he split the ribs
separated tongue from throat

perfectionist carver of the flesh
surgeon of the steak
leaning on the back of the stainless
display case, elevated
by knowledge of fat and sinew
the angled folds of white paper on rolls,
unfurled and then wrapped tight
like a swaddled infant.

somehow above us
detached by sharpened knife
on rough steel, by meat tray
and a lifetime of latching the freezer door.
tempting the slicer with the tip
of each finger, listening
to the grinder transform hunks
into curling patterns,
unrecognizable, and so close
to being alive.

Obituary for a New York Corpse

the anonymous thunk of you
aloof on the median
against the Canadian barrier
the Braille bumps dividing lanes
every vehicle accidentally
dissecting you
soul already ascended
disheartened by the very
flesh and bone of it all
the shred and burst
the tear and flattening
unrecognizable, inhuman
commuters convince themselves
you are part of a stray dog
you are only a shirt and a steak
fallen from a black garbage bag
blood is really brown paint
and you are only shadows
tricking sunrise eyes
only you know what happened
mistake or purpose
thrown or stumbled
pushed or tripped
high or suicidal
now the whole of you
simply pieces that can never fit together
a mess of DNA
a small paragraph
on the back page
of the *New York Times*

Deprivation Litany

For the place the moon should be
in this dull gray field of sagging sky,
if it were heavy enough to drop through
like a lemon, from a wet, brown paper lunch sack.

For the words I used to know,
they left while I slept, unplugged the electric blanket,
hit the snooze button on the alarm clock, stuck
dictionary pages in the toaster slots, unlocked
every door's deadbolt.

For the voice that knew the phone line,
navigated all of the wire and cable, remembered
the heavy plugs of the switchboard, the specific
vocal tone, the deep, shaking laugh.

For everything I wanted, but didn't need.
For everything I have, and never wanted.
For everything I lost, that I meant to lose.
For everything I found and put away
for later, at the back of a drawer, in the corner
of my kitchen, and between the last pages
of my grandfather's disintegrating family dictionary,
leather cover bound with electrical tape, all of the words
barely holding on.

The things that don't happen

First the stuttering, almost always
at the final word of your sentence;
although we tell you to slow down,
we really want the stubs of words
that you hack at with the dull knife
of your tongue, to be over.

We wish you wouldn't speak at all,
but we don't ever say this aloud.
Instead, we nod and pause, raise our
eyebrows, moving our own mouths
over the word, hoping it will help you
give birth to it. Verbal midwives,
coaxing and coaching, knowing
that eventually everything comes out—
screaming or silent, headfirst, ass first
or yanked by suction cups and forceps.

There is something that needs saying
and is worth the same syllable repeated
and repeated, like an odd plea
in rhythm, some Gregorian chant
of annoyance and expectation,
awaiting a decent end.

The poem I did not write

never uses upper case letters,
unless I am writing your name,
which I am not.
And that particular shade of blue
like the wall in Van Gogh's crooked bedroom,
the specific blue of a dying crocus
at the end of April; that is the blue
I will never write about.
I am certain the poem would have been
a sestina, the forgotten form, moving patterns
of repeated words, tricky litany,
to say in so many lines
I lost you.
Instead, only lined paper.
Instead, the hum of a black fan's blades.
Instead, the absence of words
that still want to be written.
White sentences erased
by the simple act of missing.

Goodbye to paper

I would write paper a letter,
mix the language into scribbles
of a vernacular that made sense,
except the paper is gone.
Where did we go wrong?
Was it the indiscriminate origami,
hundreds of folded swans
fading on my windowsill?
Was it the paper footballs,
callously flicked across the desk,
in boredom? And who decided
to turn paper into work?
The endless forms, the dead horses
painted on the flaps of envelopes,
the infinite rows of trees,
milled and pressed, each with their own
rings of stories, of forest nights
and chainsaws, of snow breaks,
and bear claw climbs, of fire wind
and pine needle silence.
Paper, forgive us,
for the picnic plates and cheap
napkins, for the stench
of ink in printers, for the abusive
light of copy machines, for the soft
bound books we throw in our bags, keep
on our nightstands, drop
in our bathtubs.

Who will I crumple now?
My tears run like blue fountain-pen ink,
like words streaming down a page, in a poem
about pauses and absence,
written on what is blank and flat,
now stained with a colored needle
below a canvas of skin.

Reunion of the Separated

You belong to a boy who rode motorcycles. My chest tightens when engines rev, my pulse keeps time with the whirs and clicks of idle motors. I put my fingers on my throat to feel the bass of this song. I thought I knew who he was then, had dreams that a boy without a helmet performed fast gravel somersaults to be inside me. The medium told me the same, she smelled motor oil when she pricked my finger to look for features in my blood. He was wearing blue, she told me, jeans with a red tag on the back pocket, black tennis shoes, a striped navy-and-white sweatshirt. Before meeting her that morning I'd purchased a blue dress. I hated blue before surgery, never wore it—I was a pinched vein then, an oxygen starved baby, short one aorta. I had to squat to push blood through my legs, up to my brain.

I found his family while researching an obituary that matched my transplant date, the day my heart shriveled in the surgeon's hands like an overripe fruit, its bruised skin concealing rotten pulp. Until that moment the organ was a *papier-mache* piñata, and every pump of blood was a swing, freeing red-wrapped candy from tearing layers. You came to me in an Igloo cooler, as inconspicuous as a six-pack of beer—all eighteen years of brown feet on cement, a healthy diaphragm yell, a love for fried chicken. Now his mother tries not to stare at my chest when she speaks. She calls him by name occasionally, reminiscing over a bike contest he won, sharing news of his sister's engagement. I show her the scar. I would let her run her finger along its satiny seam if she asked. She cries and hugs me, a reminder that you are his heart, racing.

I've been sleeping with a younger man who has tattoos on his knuckles, firm legs, and a Harley-Davidson. When our bare chests meet I am closer to him than he knows. You, pomegranate-sized stranger, beat to another that could be your twin. I can't interpret your rhythm and flutter. Are you angry you weren't sewn into a man, delighted to be sitting behind handlebars again, or is this finally the marriage of our arteries, the steady rush of possession? My doctor puts the stethoscope to my ears, and I cry listening to our knocking, to you, my secondhand muscle. Oh, to give you a voice. I am exhausted by these one-sided conversations. The cavity you fill never tried to speak before, there was only a hum where there's now your thudding murmur. Faithful partner, we touch only on the inside.

Slain American as a Piece of Paper

I am flattened, two dimensional,
as light and thin as flesh peeled
for grafting over the deepest burn.
I curl and shrink, but still ascend
in flames, afloat on wings pressed
from pulp, like any Christmas pageant angel.
Who expects this reduction?
Now I fit in your hands, a spectrum
of dots worthy of Seurat, the very
blueprint of me—wrapped on lampposts
and bulletin boards, a simple
color copy, my typeset name.
Sign your declarations on me,
encrypt your coded orders here.
I've been rolled and tied with heavy
satin ribbon, they've shredded me
in ticker tape parades. Strips
in your hair, swirling
in your streets' gutters.
You stand in cinders, your soles
melting. You inhale me
as ash and dust, the thickness
and cloud that is me,
between a gasp and a sob.

The thing I like best about you

is that you are not me,
you in the light through forest fire smoke
the gray and red, the choke and burn.
You in the lake, the green water
a meadow mimic; you leave behind
a series of Os on the surface,
tiny proof that you exist.
You with the glass eye,
like a recycled marble that once rolled
a chalk circle on playground blacktop.
You pop it out in an instant shorter
than a blink, and I am sure that iris and pupil
watch us from the bowl on the counter,
follow in the shadow, know
the empty places.
You with the folded paper in your pockets,
rubber glue on your fingertips, an ink stain
on your palm.
You with the quiet of a breath just held,
the sound of a bathtub filling
the moment before it overflows.
You with the instincts of nighttime,
the markers of the changing moon pulling
yellow light across your tides,
like pale threads on a loom.
You without any of me.

Autopsy Portrait

On a photograph of an anonymous woman, recently autopsied

The sweetness no longer matters.
It might not feel like it, but you know what is next.

You never let your gestures define you,
now is no exception.
As if chasing away invisible autumn gnats,
you swatted at the air when you laughed,
exactly as your grandmother did.
It was endearing when you caught your tongue
in your cheek, to defeat tears, as if rolling
a sugar cube around in your mouth.
Three of your toes are webbed;
you make me want to swim.

I tell myself I should be removing your stitches.
But without them you would fall apart;
the cuts are too deep, carve straight through you, pumpkin.
They weigh your meaty liver on a scale
that should instead measure the pounds
of a new baby, or several cups of sugar.
The human body as filet.
Still, you are undeniably beautiful in your sleeping stretch.
No twitch or yawn, no flush of naked embarrassment,
camera shy does not apply to you.
I sense that at any moment, awakened,
you will explain the gore of this costume,
these unnatural patterns that refuse to heal.
Tell me it is movie blood, special effects,
a convincing temporary tattoo.

Your body, transformed into patchwork needlecraft.
Your scars, a new map of blue roads,
a mess of dead ends and desert skin,
not enough water, lacking borders,
dreaming of explorers in canoes who know
exactly where to find you.

Lies

You are artificial sweetener
white and silent,
untested and toxic,
the light powder coating everything:
candied volcano ash.

You are the smiling doctor
wearing safety goggles and the latex gloves
I am allergic to.
Anaesthetized, I still feel everything.
My paralyzed mouth surrenders
to the scream in my eyes.
You crack my chest
and spread my ribs
with skill, practice, precision,
so much less blood than I expected.

I am not your experiment.
Instead I am a revelation:
this freeway system of corpuscles,
the shy white bones,
the strings of sinew that resist reaching,
the miracle of persevering synapses,
the little telegrams my brain sends my heart, a heart
that waits like a war widow at her front door,
unable to open the latch, to swing the brass hinges
to a place where she can see straight ahead—
beyond the shoulders of a uniformed chaplain—
into the world that is left.

Painless

A simple gift, from a godmother who misplaced her pouch of fairy dust. No golden glitter landed in sparkles on my head. She failed to wrap a leather Bible in tissue, or give me a wooden music box covered in sharp shells and blue sea glass. Here, she says, offering her empty palms, may you never feel pain.

I am discovered. A mass of beauty bruises, lengths of ribbon scars, imprint and incision, all scabs before they can heal. I raced my wooden wagon into trees, jumped from shed roof to trampoline, rode the zip line into the garage wall. It is not injury that I crave, but contact, the wounding moment. Adrenaline is my shocked audience, swallowing her cry, never screaming.

What I have become: defiant, senseless, willing to reach into a shrunken garden volcano erupting with fire ants. I watch them trail bits of my skin to their queen, small attempts to steal my fingerprints. My blood, tiny velvet robes painted on divided bodies, dancing in a trail.

Look for the signs: display me under a fluorescent light, examine me. I am the forgotten masterpiece, roped off with velvet, alarmed. Hang me if you'd like. See my thick brushstrokes and layered pigment. No one wants to touch me until I'm crooked or fallen. Knock me down please.

The truth is: you cannot hurt me, nor do the stitches I pull out with my teeth, or the skin fused in band-aids, not even the sores that open and close like summer poppies. I am my own anesthetic—always numb. The future is worry. What sparks will disfigure me? How deep can the blade be pushed in? Will I have a tendency towards shirtless men who will beat me? Will I tour the world with needles in my eyes? Will my answer always be yes?

Sound

I hear worms turning as they bury themselves in soil. I awaken to the sound of a plum's skin shedding. The inhaling and exhaling of birds distracts me; their blue lungs boom as they fill with sky. I hear your muscles contract, snap like elastic, cramp into fists the size of baking apples. The veins in your wrists call to my heart, a syncopated code that says, "I'm in charge, you follow me."

In the morning there is nothing left of you but an imprint on the featherbed. Your outline reminds me of traced hands, Thanksgiving art projects in grammar school, fingers as feathers, thumb as head. Your giant thumbprint is set in the pillow beside me, the place your legs thrashed outside the comforter is plumage. I want to fill the space you left with plaster, to twist pipe cleaners around tissue flowers and commemorate your resting place. I want to hear memory fix itself with each popped bubble, as it dries. I want to capture each stirring of you.

What I do hear is a cat's spiny tongue catching hair and ticks, filtering out fluff and grime, the sound of cleansing and bristles. I hear my fingernails grow as they tap against glass, a steady creak against the cuticles, a tearing. I hear the moonlight through your skin, a glinty rhapsody of xylophones and tapped champagne glasses, all light notes, never a sharp or flat.

Falling Senseless

For Carter Cooper

It's as if I'm wearing falconer's gloves, but I am leather—
thick, worn, yet never pierced through. Once I was a living cow's hide
enduring a straw-covered August hillside, without a single oak
to graze beneath. Now there are no senses in my fingertips,
not a tingle numb, not paralysis; it's just that when I touch
nothing registers: not the scorch of my morning shower,
not the bay wind—it only blows over my hair, pushes me.
Not my sheets pulled across my feet, tucked too tightly in the corners,
not the velvet cushions on Mother's music room loveseat.
A kiss is torture, there is no pressure behind it, and I have nothing
to give back. My sense of taste slips as well, trips on my teeth,
scarring my tongue. I salt everything, but I am never thirsty.
I can no longer smell coffee, or bus exhaust. I open a bottle
of vanilla, a jug of ammonia, a tin of pipe tobacco. Nothing. Only
an odorless haze and a vague memory of my father's aftershave.
My hearing hasn't improved, although the sound of my own pulse
distorts other noises. Once I listened to each of Mother's swallows,
could enjoy the piano two blocks away through open windows,
a student practicing Bach's *Requiem*, and the chains from park swings
just across the street, their specific squeak and rattle, dragging
in the wind. Even when I am not asleep, my eyes won't fully open.
I no longer have peripheral vision. Every read sentence blurs,
and the portraits Mother hung years ago are now just paint
patterns that run down the walls, as if they are trying to escape
their frames. For now, the only connection I have to anything
is gravity.

*Carter's final words, said to his mother, Gloria Vanderbilt, just before he
jumped off of her Manhattan balcony, were: "Will I ever feel again?"*

My four favorite bones

Femur is first, for the sound
itself—for its solid line and thick
whiteness, an inner crutch, a length,
a height.

The first vertebra, like a precious ivory clasp,
linking latch, connecting and supporting,
a spinal handshake, upright
and forward, the captain
of the cord, steady and about to salute.

Every phalange, delicacy and downfall,
thin, pale twig, covered in knots,
allows me to grip and drop, gather
the persimmons, address the last note, doodle
a star, mysterious under a glove of skin, talking
through cracked knuckles.

Isn't the skull the biggest? Its dome
of glory, a living helmet, a suitcase
for a string of words, folded
and packed into soft tissue
that pulses—like dying stars, the flickers
that command. *Get up and walk, you
have an itch, blink now.* There is a sound
inside—from the beat of blood and the buzz
of synapses—that is the bone
of the poem.

Thought upon Waking

Instead of a thought, instead of the closing
credits of the dream I've already forgotten, just a vague
blurry reel, names scrolling down on a black background,
written in a dead language, untranslatable.
Instead of a warm breath trapped against winter sheets,
flannel and down, that first eye opened, the face
of the clock, glowing green, an ornament to morning.
Instead of feet on the floor, the padded shuffle
to the bathroom, water running like blue ribbons
let loose from the tap. Instead of the sigh of rising,
the heater thumping on, like a short knock
on a wooden door, an arrival. Instead of a thought,
a resistance to it. A refusal to accept. More sleep,
instead. In the quiet of before light, in the moon
that will not set, in the wind that blows
all doors closed. Sleep.

The Suspicious Grieving

They cry too much in public
clutching damp handkerchiefs,
wadded up white surrender flags
flown around red noses and baggy eyes.

They drink too much.
Look at all of the empty red-wine bottles
in their curbside recycling bin, next to
the aluminum tins from the casseroles
of knocking neighbors and coworkers,
so much lasagna and baked chicken with rice.

They don't get out enough.
Their bathrobes are too heavy, chenille
and terry cloth, pulling their shoulders down,
back into bed, where the sheets
still smell of him or her—the dandruff
shampoo, the cocoa butter lotion. Tangible
and present, but absent still.

Did I mention that they are behind in the laundry?
Their bills are late. The grass grows twice as fast
as it used to. Their written lists lengthen
from the paper onto the table, the ink
smudges. The TV is always on, and the sink
water continuously runs over dirty dishes.

They leave a trail of Kleenex, of letters,
of pieces of envelopes and bent photographs; the evidence
is everywhere. They are dragging endless
tracks in their carpeted hallways, leaving behind
fingerprints, DNA, follicles. They won't get out
of the shower. They refuse to drive
into town; they just sit in the car's front seat,
keys dangling from the ignition, about to turn
the engine on, about to put a foot on the gas pedal,
about to shed their shoes, their clothes, their hair
and their skin, simultaneously—eyes closed,
all at once hidden and revealed.

Broken

The truth lies
only partly in the details:
the stray blue thread of her fraying shawl,
the wink of a scar above her left eye,
and the soft red leather shoes,
red because they have been dyed
with her blood.

They bend her limbs
in late spring, when sap
is the heaviest, when blooms turn
from almosts to true buds.

They bruise her
a new shade of blue,
not as hopeful as beach glass,
or the shimmer of lapis wedding eye shadow.

Her blossoms spread
beneath the skin, like tattoos
that have melted.

The snap of her bones,
like branches breaking before
they land on snow. Splitting
the air with an unexpected crack,
the kind of sound that makes you wish
you didn't have ears, that falls
silent immediately, like
the color white, the same color
as a waving, surrender flag.

The blue in her blood
hides behind the red.
She wishes she had a hide,
like the elephants wearing gold bells
on their saddles that she saw
in the parade with her father
when she was newly ten.

She tries imagining her skin
as the petals of pink oleanders,
their beauty permeated by toxicity:
poisonous seeds, sap, and root.

She pictures her insides
as an unfurling bolt of embossed silk,
embroidered in silver thread.
Work that was done by hand,
in a dark room, late at night,
by a woman who stitched in silence, purely
out of practice and memory.
What she knows by touch and counts alone
is never lost.

Where will they find the pieces?

Scattered on the snow like old typewriter keys
and blackened red ribbon, looping almost letters
out-of-order words.
Or hunks of meat in plastic, bound with silver tape,
stacked in a garage's upright freezer beside root beer
popsicles and a frosted-over lasagna.
Perhaps poured into a backyard patio, just under
the pebbled surface, an underground mosaic
of limb and length.
Maybe there will be only a sliver of bone,
charred by the fire pit, a tiny elephant tusk,
an ivory toothpick, an ashen exclamation point,
stripped of its dot.
Or out to sea, like an honored soldier, slid
like a beer across a wet mahogany bar, off the starboard edge.
Transformed into bubbles, an odd anemone,
the flesh-colored coral that is now just another part
of the oceanic ecosystem, kissed by fish
then left to brine.
It will probably be the forest, with its dark
open mouth of shifting earth, its bark teeth
and fern skin, the lure of a trail, sketched clearly
in the foreground, the safety of sunlight,
and a deep patch of soil, newly turned
and packed, in an unnatural clearing.

Ex Vivo

For my husband, misdiagnosed with a malignant tumor

I never thought of you in terms of cells,
the dark bars' shadow stripes across countless
trapped nuclei, the microscopic prisons, inaudible
sounds of invisible tin cups dragging back and forth
over metal rows.

You are like a fish they cut the hook out of,
startling in this unfamiliar air, connected
by a tight, clear line. Drink drops of blood
from your own lip, taste the salty newness of removal,
miss the sliver of you, lost to a blade and specimen jar.

This threatening mass, flesh-toned, the size
of a pin's head, is dissected in layers.
The top tissue is adulthood and paperwork, the tugs
of small hands. Lines from spoken words
try to write deeply above your mouth, where your lip
meets skin, at the margins of our kisses.
Beneath the surface, deeper red, where the fears
of your childhood escape from an incision:
hippies, teenagers with syringes, your dad in the hospital
for months. Pulled together, a new seam
of whiskers and matching black thread.

The hole in you, now pink and closed,
fades in weeks, as if it had always been there, another piece
of who you are now. Your quiet story is of a costumed cell,
wearing a dark cape and black mask, with veiny eyes
and jaundiced skin, now just a figment on a slide, a shadow
masquerading as a thunder cloud.

The Suicide Poem

> For Jeanette S.

How many birthdays has it been
since you decided to stop aging?
The November Hudson Bay, all foam row,
bleached hull, gray water, gulls, and black skyline.
The repeated song of a rudder's broken churn.
What became of your blonde locks, worn straight
and clean? Did suds bubble where you submerged,
the tiny pops of your frozen breaths, the pale palms
of your winter hands, without gloves, waving
and lost in the wake?
You were never found.
Not in pieces, not whole, no stray scarf threads,
no leopard-skin pocketbook, thick
with tiny, water-warped photos.
Not the length and life of you, the brilliance
and depth, just the permanent turning
of the swells, your last sounds swallowed
in graceful spins of final descent, beneath
the unbearable above.

I have no right to grieve you

> For Will Norton, who was killed in the Joplin, Missouri,
> tornado, May 22, 2011

still, I want to try on your red-lined, black felt coat,
two sizes too small, and as heavy as chainmail.
I will wear it around and see if anyone asks me,
is *that yours?* It must be difficult to move
through the air of day, the blind and bright
of it, to take off your skin at night and lay it beside
your bed, curled in a heap like a sleeping dog.
And if you place it on a scale, this sadness cannot register
a measureable weight. It needs a platform
larger than the one used for the city zoo's elephant.
Although at first this burden makes you shrink and float,
because it is too real, but is invisible to everyone else,
this helium poison. And having to face each waking
without your exhale into this world of deceptive,
ever-present air, and this crooked backdrop of dawn,
and the open shattered sky, makes me want to
put "un" before every word that I speak,
and every word that I hear:
undream, unsearch, ungrasp, ungasp,
unmissing, unagony, unyesterday, unseparate, unlose,
unmemory, untiming, unfollow, unask, unfind,
ungreen-fury sky, unshambles, unsorrow, unforget,
unabsent, unshredded, unheavy, unmourn, undespair,
untoday, uneverything, undo, undo, undo.

What do you choose?

A fist closed around a staggered bouquet of cut straws,
like stems without their blooms,
striped red and white,
reminding you of childhood,
cherry snow cone syrup, movie
soda cups, the sweet stretch of open
Pixie Stix. It smells like July; there is
the trace scent of sulfur from a burning sparkler,
bubbles in hot pavement, chlorine in the tips
of your ponytails. The short straw loses,
as we compare lengths, debate
the order with which this loss was chosen.
A number between one and ten.
Eeeny, meany, miney, moe.
The winner gets the last fudgsicle,
the best sleeping bag, a seat
beside the birthday girl at dinner.
The loser gets a tiny plastic cup of ice cream,
crusted with ice crystals, and a flat wooden spoon
that really scrapes rather than scoops.
The loser gets the thin comforter, the couch pillow,
a spot on the floor by the bathroom door, where girls
trip over her head throughout this summer night.
This is not so much a choice as a bad draw.
Although she pulled on the straw, and accepted
defeat, sometimes we don't really get to choose.
If given the choice, she may have picked
at least one victory, one slumber-party luxury;
she might have been the one photographed in the dim light
of trick candles, in a photo where she is holding the cake,
in that last minute before the wish.

A question that you should say yes to

Is the asking
more important than the question? What if
you forget to raise your voice
at the end of the sentence, like
a heavy kite tail, over-tied with ribbons,
no wind in the meadow?
If you had only asked me, if I
had only said, Is this a question?
Instead, the statement sat on the table
between us, a tiny, tarnished
trophy, both sets of our hands on its base.
What does the plaque say? Who wins
this award?
Just ask me.
And if I say yes, or nod, I will still
ask you to repeat the question. I like
the tones in your throat, the threads you
string the words on, and saying things
over makes them real.
Say it again.
Ask me.
I can't even think
of the letters that spell
no when I hear your voice.

1976 Gonzales, California

This is not Italy, not these golden hills
tangled with the reaches of oak
that click with worms at the end of summer.
Two rows of eucalyptus trees line a dirt road.
The air is dry dust, tastes like the color brown.
Our fingernails are packed with farm dirt.
As we walk between perfectly spaced tree towers,
their pods fall like oxidized amusement park tokens,
thrown from a pier by a child, now washed
into barnacle beauties—rough and scented.

The pomegranate tree, shoulders sloped,
arms weighted, is dressed in heavy spots,
a rash of red. Every hanging circle is more
than an ornament, each is a swollen berry
ripe with its own secret fruits.
When halves are torn, two clusters of crimson
arils stain our chins and fingertips
a more delicate shade of blood,
the lipstick of childhood.

Bad Girl

She leaves the dance early,
straddles the bleachers
in Wrangler jeans
she had to lie down to pull on,
the pockets pushed down
with a wooden-handled ice pick.

She pulls a boy behind her,
as if he were a blindfolded hostage.
Her stride is always forward—
those pointed boot tips,
her stamped silver name spelled on her belt,
the closest thing she could get to a tattoo,
at sixteen.

The rest was left up to us:
what we knew or heard,
what we guessed and created.
The issue of the small flask,
how the backseat vinyl squeaked
beneath them, how she ever managed
to take off those jeans and put them on again.

She came back to the dance
at eleven p.m.,
waited for her mother
in the school parking lot,
like any other girl,
flushed from dancing,
wanting to keep a secret.

An inebriated monk illuminating a great text

The damp end of my sable brush, golden.
My teeth stained with cheap red table wine, consecrated
blood, or any deep liquid forgotten in a wooden chalice.
The entirety of my duty is replication, exacted
and measured in the increments of my drunkenness.
My gift from God: a steady hand. This brush, dipped
in jewel-toned paint, dragging down the manuscript
reminds me of a woman rising from the bath,
her hair in a point on her bare back.
These are not unholy figments; it is necessary
that I stay awake, find and interpret text
in candlelit silence. The only sounds: my swallowing,
scraping parchment, the occasional dropped palette.
I slur a prayer for better eyesight as I serve,
outlining His letters, following the Word.
My confession is that loneliness has wed despair
in a poorly lit, unattended ceremony, and now
my penance is the proper comma, again and again,
the shape of a bleeding stigmata. My salvation—
knowing when to lift the brush handle
and sleep.

The cellist's lament

The cello makes me sad.
Her wood burled and worn,
her big hips cocked to one side.
So tired of being restrung and rubbed,
exhausted by the smell of resin.
She is always leaning back,
as if caught in a mime's wind
gone on a moment too long, although
she has always been limbless and resigned
to the control of another's hands.

But her neck still rests on my shoulder,
and she likes to pretend that we are two winter birds,
left to the tangles of neighborhood threads,
dryer lint, birthday ribbon, and twigs
lost from the peeling birch tree.

And we are not so much hiding, as huddling,
and we are not so much afraid, as determined.

And together, apart from the wind
and the clustering scraps of circling air
and frozen water that paint every limb white,
we share music in the silence: low, like the deepest
lake ice before it cracks on the surface,
thrumming and lush, muffled and insulated.

Until spring, when on this ground, no longer white
like stacked paper sheets scattered with black notes,
another song is written, and the soil
turns and greens, and everything underneath
means something new.

Turbulence

Surely, the overhead compartments, heavy plastic and hinged,
will all pop open.
Not unlike a forced blossom in a green house,
a green curl that is suddenly an orchid, surprised white,
opened faster than an envelope.
And the irony is, the turbulence
is really only pockets of air.
There are no geese pureed in the engine blades, sudden
feather clouds and trailing smoke, a cartoon tragedy.
The pilots are only slightly drunk, could do this
in their sleep, which we've been told
they have actually done.
This is not comforting.
So we bounce, suspended in a metal, pressurized cabin,
trusting the thrusters, our faith in the religion of landing
gear opening and locking into place, assured
that the orange oxygen masks rarely dangle,
are really only a prop for a movie once filmed here.
But it feels like we're hitting asteroids, and the nylon carry-ons
are restless, the bottled toiletries, hostile
and swelling, even the zippers are edgy.
The seatbelt sign is on, that sad, red, glowing figure,
forever strapped in place.
As if a fabric belt can save us from the sky,
and the altitude we were never meant to survive in.
There should be an emergency light that displays
a pair of lungs, with the command, "Try to breathe."
All of this blue, and these invisible crashes,
and the little trays we lock into place,
we have something better than this.

But do not be mistaken, we are in flight now.
We are no more than a weight in this cloud, closer
than we ever will be to the stars, even though they die and fall,
gray weights that burn out, like the final seconds
of a cigarette, like church candlewicks drowning
in white wax, like last words that want to shine.

Twister

For Tracy Presslor, Will Norton's aunt

The walls are breathing,
perhaps even panting, from attempting to run.
And when you say spinning, I prefer
to imagine the spangled motion of a figure skater
wearing a silver blur that is a sequined body suit.
I would choose the simplicity of making myself dizzy
with childhood friends on a damp June lawn,
staring at the dusk, an orange floating in blue water.
Now, there is no time to hide, no cellar door,
no cast iron bathtub, no storm shelter cinderblock.
There is only the sound of the wind of knives,
of the merciless pulling apart, the unnerving rattles
of endings and foundations, the cracking
of treetops and bones, and the endless fields
of glass, as if the pieces are a crop needing harvest.
These are the shreds and shards,
the empties, the hollows, the quiet nothings.
There is no here here, and no here
there, either. There is only
the used to be and the maybe
someday, once again.

Middle Name

My initial response is to say, you are second string,
a clear, taut line, one of many necessary for a guitarist
to play a chord. You are just a plink when alone.
You are not a middle child, though you sit like one—
quiet, with your legs crossed, glancing back and forth
between the real sounds of a first name called,
and the slick permanence of the last name.
You are usually reduced to a letter, you will end up in therapy.
You are often short because you have to be, an angry,
monosyllabic stump of a word, longing to be said.
You are often uttered only in anger, or by command.
You've been labeled and typecast, like a once favorite
sitcom star failing in a new series because you are too familiar.
Tiny tag-a-long, I didn't choose you, you were an afterthought
in a hospital room, from a book my mother thumbed through.
I never needed you, not the cursive version, not in type,
not printed on tan paper with fat pencils in kindergarten.
That is why you fell from the order, dropped from a height
that broke you in three places. I don't feel guilty
for not missing you, I filled the space you left with a name
that is my center—decided with a checkmark on a form.
I was never your mother or your child, you were just stuck
to me, like clothes pulled onto wet skin, like pine sap
on the palms of my hands, like an overplayed song's bad refrain,
a part of something else I always wanted to shed.

Learning About Trees

Notice first that they are tall, beyond
the power poles that bend and spark
under the weight of January snow.
The trees know their yoga, have stretched
and bowed only to return square shouldered,
in proper posture.

Please recognize the deep moles, blackened
by lightning strikes, in the thick bark
that was once sapling skin
now ragged and squirrel-abused, a home
and a maypole and a scratching post.

Most of the roots are hidden, bulging
wooden veins. They hold trees to the ground,
heavy, primitive ship anchors,
eventually rusting and rotting through.

When the trees are old enough they fall
because their insides are now beetles,
or the wind shifts to the north,
or there is not enough water,
or the late winter soil is too drenched
and has to let go.

You've already seen the diagram,
know the arrows' path, all of that oxygen
and carbon dioxide. And you've read
that slim green book about a boy
who sold his tree in pieces
and ended up old on a stump.

This isn't to warn you, but just to let you know,
that sometimes they outlive the people in their shade,
with their wide trunks and mysterious rings
and treetop perspective. Sometimes they burn,
cracking and shaking hands, in a bluster of sparks.
Sometimes people carve letters into them,
a scar they cannot read, in a language
that is not their own.

In a Goddamn Hotel Room

>   For Eugene O'Neill

The wallpaper peels like sunburnt skin;
errant patches of brown paint show through
where spots of red flocking were half glued.
A basin sits on your bureau, the pitcher a dull
blue, the color of your fingertips, stained
with ink from your fountain pen's gold nib.
The pine wardrobe wears the dents of someone
else's familiarity; its doors refuse to close,
like your sleeping mouth. White fringe
from the carpet's fraying edges lies
curled on the wooden floor like scattered worms waiting
to crawl beneath your sheets and sleep
in your eyes. Scentless, foreign cloth
encircles you. Your wife's ginger powder, the mint-
colored cologne you slapped under your chin, soap
flakes smelling of eucalyptus that sometimes stuck
in the pockets of your pants—all are
absent. The nightstand's marble top has chipped
corners. You keep a glass there, half filled
with murky Scotch, smudged with your damp fingerprints.
You reach for it in your sleep, spill on a letter
you ended, "A love that knows, Eugene."

Your eyes open to cracked plaster, and you remember
where you were born, the hotel at Broadway and 43rd. Your mother
took you once, to the room where she stained a mattress
silent maids covered minutes later with whiter sheets.
Your mother laughed when you asked her if she paid extra
for registering as one and leaving as two. You think
of when you checked in a week ago, barely able to sign your name,
leaning against the mahogany counter. You know you will
check out today on a stretcher, as nothing. It will not be
the first time you were carried through a hotel's front doors.

How do you choose your dying words? Are they a line you saved,
too perfect for stage direction? As you enunciate each
syllable, are you actor or writer? Your face tightens
with rehearsed pain, your voice rises
with the final anger of leading men. You close
your life like you once closed theater curtains,
with one swift gesture, in this last place
that is not your own.

Take it back,

> For Christine Lompa

this band of sapphires, set
in platinum, that I would wear
down to the thickness of thread,
or catch on my bureau's handle.
In thirty years it would slide off,
when I'm elbow deep
in potting soil, and I'd have to pour
our backyard through my sifter,
waiting for a clink or glint.
You'd have to replace me
with a woman who moves slowly, her big knuckles
armed with leather work gloves, and
the habit of touching thumb to fourth finger.
My dress, already vacuum-sealed in plastic,
is the casualty of plans, a shelved specimen
of my taste for imported lace, fabric-
covered buttons, that my mother will keep
next to boxes of sailor suits, bunny pajamas,
a christening dress for her inconceivable
grandchild. Some will say I have bad
circulation, not enough blood to heat
my heart and feet; others will ask if I cried
while canceling the hall with high ceilings,
one hundred tables covered with wheat-colored cloth,
six women in matching silk who already call me
by your last name, ivory-paneled invitations
in bold antique Roman, and arrangements of tulips
tied with French ribbons, bows holding forever
in permanent wire knots. The date will pass

like Saturdays in August do; I will rise and open
windows to the morning smell of summer heat
about to be. I will trap the last cool air, slide shut
glass panes with latches, flip white shutters closed.
On my afternoon walk I will pop bubbles
in the street's soft tar, the sun hot enough
to fade bougainvillea, to burn
away the color of photographs,
from true to one tone of gray.

Yosemite Fall

If there had been no wine,
the same deep red as the peaking Virginia Creeper
writing Fall words up the granite face.
Wine served in a plastic cup from a stack,
leaving wet rings in the dirt,
perfect circles refilled and spilled again.
If there had been no glare on the camera lens,
that unforgiving spotlight
of September sun at noon.
If the balance of our bodies' design had been the rule,
two feet always planted at a shoulder's distance,
weight in the heels, steady as the water
rushing patterns across drowned rocks.
One misstep decides everything.
If only there had been something to cling to.
In descent, his outstretched hands
held only slick moss, the cold foam of surface water,
a mess of loose twigs.
Though they found him at the bottom,
broken from flight, from being dropped
like a heavy plum from a high branch, bruised
and washed into smooth pieces, still we
look to the air, still we lean out
to peer over the edge.

J.M. Barrie

It was over when he learned of mortal wounds,
a seven-year-old with a dead brother
whose perfect head had split on the ice,
like a peach thrown against a window.
His childhood, given over to dark
clothing, a heavy trench coat of guilt,
Wellingtons of grief. If there's one thing
losing prepares us for, it's more loss.
His ink and words, like homemade wrapping
paper, the sparkle and dressing
his own life lacked, tied tightly
enough to cut fingers tearing
knotted twine, forgetting the army knife
always in his trousers' pocket.
The lost boys, his adopted sons,
like his own brother—sudden spaces
on a page, every gap between things, from the hole
in the O, to that lonely hollow
curling just to the left of a question mark.
He was never young. Where did he go
to write? How could he hide?
A child behind a tree in a garden,
his eyes closed and covered,
waiting to be found.

Honeymoon

For Elenora Annable, my maternal grandmother

It was a time before the shortage of bees,
when the beekeeper, in a silver mesh veil
and white canvas gown, found the hives
overrun with combs and queens, patterns like lace.
Before the bees faded, lost the color of the daffodil
in early spring, before their bodies dulled to gray, no longer
darkened with stripes as black as an open mouth
on a moonless night.

In only three days, her boxes were unpacked.
She put away the starched linens that were once her mother's
mother's, she hung five dresses on wooden hangers, stacked
the white plates from a department store hundreds of miles from her
address. In only three days, days of placement,
skin, paper, and cigarette smoke, days of drawn
curtains, days spent washing and pressing,
while the chicken roasted, and the bread dough rose
under a thick cotton dishtowel, she was undone.
Undone like her bodice laces, like her Sunday school boots,
like the last notes of jazz on the Victrola, like pieces of a bird's
nest that blew from a sycamore branch to the brick walk
leading to their front door. She was not yet used to putting his name
after hers, although she had written it for years, secretly.
She waited until she was 18, and there they were, beside
each other, in the last moments before sleep, in the almost
light of a moon's sliver, cutting a slice in the sky,
between the curtains.

In only three days, she knew about the other woman.
"That woman" was her name. "That woman
doesn't love you," she said. "You didn't marry her."
In that moment, when she should have folded her life
back into boxes and refastened the straps
on that new leather suitcase, when she should have run
down the street, swinging summer sleeves,
brushing rose bushes, so clouded with the hum of bees,
she only turned her body and walked into the kitchen, lit a burner,
tied her apron strings, and remembered how beautiful he was
when he danced.

The right way to say goodbye

She leaves the motor running
not intending to end her own life,
but if she has to die to kill him,
so be it.

She leaves the motor running
not to warm the engine or fight frost,
not to hear its starting clicks, like fast spikes
in a footrace, the sound of a loud sprint
on pavement.

She leaves the motor running,
swings open the side door, and she is ajar.
Her ankles give way. She stretches out
on concrete, posed like a '40s movie siren
on a lake rock, delicate and still
in her modest bathing suit.

She leaves the motor running,
breathing exhausted, useless air.
In the fumes she sees the shapes
of every letter that spelled his hard words,
each one outlined and weighted—the color
of smoke from burning tires.

She leaves the motor running,
while he sleeps across the vinyl bench seat,
the place he crawled from the bar curb.
He tried to hit her while she drove,
and his drunk aim left her hunched, flinching.

She leaves the motor running,
staying for the finality of it.

She waits a moment too long, a second
the length of a kiss.
How many times had they slept
in the same room after a fight?
She, in a heap on the floor
like an overcoat that missed the hook.
He, unwound, heavy limbs outstretched
in solid sleep—the kind that comes
fast and dark to those who don't know
how to forgive or regret.

What we wear in the snow

The first layer, the closest, like water
with its surface skimmed by circles of moon, pale
like winter skin itself, not at all the orange-colored crayon
children use to fill in round faces in self-portraits.
Soft wool socks, like two skinned rabbits, sliding pelts,
some kind of foot disguise to fool the ankles,
calm the boot tongue.
Then the fleece, from a factory, not a sheep—
no tangles of hay, no shearing, no pink insides
of ears—just manufactured warmth,
run through machines that stitch and hem
the way our grandmother once did, as the kitchen windows
ran with beads of steam and the radiator hummed, as she touched
the pedal up and down on the yellow linoleum.
The head, a swaddled infant, our fists
in tiny, down punching bags. We bring a red scarf
to leave in the yard, now too tight on the throat
of a man made of three rolled sections, snow forced
onto snow, pushed harder than our arms into coat sleeves,
held together by the cold itself—the moment before water
becomes solid ice, the moment after the falling snow turns
to air that used to be snowing.

Maxine remembers the goats

Once she had been able to tell time
by the tone of their bleating.
Five goats in a pen, siblings, bought for her
to be raised for 4-H. As kids, they were loud
and long. Maxine and her sister dressed them
in baby clothes, named them after their mother's favorite
soap opera characters. They would eat anything.
Each day the girls would bring something new
to try—buttermilk soap, pencils, shoestrings,
hunks of liver, foil candy wrappers, fingernail clippings.
The goats entertained in their simple goat way.
They would not fetch a tennis ball, or curl up
on the screened porch bed for a nap with Maxine. One day
the goats were in the house, chewing the paper snowflakes
hung from fishing line across the hearth, a scattering of red
and green Monopoly houses, handfuls of dryer lint. They were wearing
Maxine's old dresses, now too small, even for her sister,
their floral patterns faded from hand-me-down existence.
At this moment, for the first time, Maxine could imagine herself
as a mother. That is until her own mother returned,
early from the market, finding goat shit
on the kitchen linoleum, and Erica Kane
swallowing a five-dollar bill from a bowl by the front door.
Soon after, the goats were gone, sold to a neighbor.
Maxine realized that she liked only the idea of goats,
remembering them.

The ability to forget

(for a woman who is mentally incapable of forgetting any detail of her life)

I cannot let go,
in my hand-beaded, red Spandex
bodysuit, my chalky grip on the trapeze handle—
blistered and weighted by my own minute details,
heavy and swinging, a pointless pendulum.

I smell syrup on pancakes and I am in a diner
with my father, who drinks five cups of coffee
before he can say he is leaving.
There is a grease stain on the left cuff
of his blue shirtsleeve. A box of cigarettes
lies open on the gray formica table. The bill,
written in blue ink, says ten dollars.
I eat whipped butter with a spoon and refuse
to look up at him. It is 9:30 on Saturday,
June 28th, 1979. I am going to swim later
with my best friend Diane at the public pool.
We meet at noon, the light is free from shadows,
it smells like hot pine needles and dirt.
I carry a denim backpack and the contents are:
a salami-and-cheese sandwich, a bag of Fritos,
a banana, and a can of Pepsi. I am fourteen
and the lifeguard is a tan college boy, whose name
is Jim. I do not want to talk.
I hold my breath under water for two minutes.
I hold my breath the entire length of the pool.
After swimming twenty laps, I spread myself out
on an orange-and-white-striped beach towel.

I am thinking it would be better somewhere
outside of myself. I cannot forget my father's
sentences. He never looked at me.
I want to speak a foreign language.
I wish I could live my life in reverse and erase
one memory after another. Like a pink-tipped pencil,
capable and ordinary, slowly rubbed down
to nothing.

I am not kissing you

Not after the car door closes, by porch light,
while my mother watches from behind shuttered windows.
She flips the switch off and on, her particular
strobe warning. I will not kiss you this summer midnight
by streetlight or headlight, the moon above us
an infinite white wish encircled by patterns of stars
that spell your name. They flicker and scatter behind clouds
before anyone else can read their letters.

I am not kissing you.
I am not holding you either.
I am not writing your name in the margins.

I am not kissing you
on empty train tracks in the rain, beside
a brick station where my suitcases fill with water.
I am not kissing you on a downhill trolley
with miracle brakes, not in a meadow
of mountain misery, and definitely not
in the tiny backseat of your car
at a drive-in movie.

I am not kissing you
for the sake of the kiss itself.
I am not kissing you
until you kiss me first.
I am not kissing you
goodbye, it will always be
hello instead.
Hello, the taste of you.
Hello, teeth and gums.
Hello pucker, hello swoon.

I am not kissing you
until I can end this poem.
Set down my heavy pen.
This is the breath before
a kiss, the opposite of a sigh.

The Narrator

I could give you my word,
which here is not a promise,
but the actual bumping of letters' elbows
as they wait in line to make sense, breaking
endless white space into beginnings and endings.

You hear my voice already, a woman
with a Southern accent in a linen blouse,
or perhaps I sound like that actor
in the insurance commercial, deep and familiar tones,
like an old felt car coat.

I give my characters to you, although
I stood in their closets just this morning,
pairing funeral suits with pointed wingtips,
pulling up girdles one leg at a time,
letting the hangers fall as they collapse
in their underwear, sobbing.
These strangers, now family to me—
their idiosyncrasies that I loathe and invent,
from their scars to their tone of voice—
usually both are raised and hidden, internal
or incessant. My words turned flesh
have brought me now to you.

So I must ask, what is my word?

I sit in the shade of this dogwood tree
with a pen, and you stare at my photo
on the back of this book, read the short
paragraph of my biography. Already
you imagine that I ate toast with jam for breakfast,
that I cannot sleep on Sunday nights,
and that I always put my knives away
in the drawer at night. My word
is simply, "yours."

Waiting for a sign

A wet-nosed fox, framed in a pane
of my French-door window,
blinks and then licks the glass.
The stereo turns on at midnight,
playing songs backwards; reverse melodies
whisper cryptic notes of what should be done.
If I knew what the signs meant—
my first name written twice on an address label,
all of the numbers on my grocery receipt, the same,
five ones in a row. And what do I make of the brown patterns
on this tortilla? Is it an apostle washing the feet of Jesus
or is he clipping his own toenails? Perhaps there is a factory
where they design marble statues with tear ducts, invent
shadow decals of the Virgin Mary to sneak onto stained glass.
Are they still signs if they are manufactured?
It is not about what they show us, but what we do
about them. This famous piece of toast, a perfect
burnt depiction of the Last Supper, wrapped
in cotton, behind glass, displayed on a fireplace mantle
surrounded by red votive candles. The miracle
is that someone saw the seated figures, before
they could be heavily buttered and devoured.

The important poem

The important thing about the poem
is that it is there.
It's true that it was waiting, sleeping
face-to-face with another poem,
on the shelf of that bookstore.

Yes, the poem is written rows,
it usually has a steady left margin,
sometimes freckled with punctuation,
other times nude and swirling down the page
like a child waving a satin ribbon
on a stick.

And then there's the issue of what it says,
comparing skin to *papier-mache* layers,
arguing that sunlight's shadows
hide things from the moon.
You must never forget what it says.

The important thing about the poem
is that someone will read it,
and someone will carry around a line,
like a tiny gold locket that he opens and shuts
without even noticing he is doing so.

Still, the most important thing about the poem
is that it is there, and now,
it is yours.

Witness

A can of spray starch sits on a stained
blue ironing board.
The shower steam sounds like shushing.
A casement window is cranked open
in tiny spins of a wrist.
There will be slices of bacon
and heavily buttered sourdough toast.
The coffee pot is returned to its maker,
a spoon rests in a chipped porcelain mug,
a yolky sun spreads over the black sky
of a cast-iron frying pan.
Everyday brown shoes have darker soles
and laces, thin leather suspenders
hold down a stiff white oxford shirt
with a gray-striped tie.
He carries a pocket street map, a worn black briefcase,
and a Bible that curves in his hand.
When he sets it on the nightstand each evening
it still curls, as if arching its back before sleep.

What is left to our determination:
the dread of unsolicited knocking,
enthusiasm for a pattern of words
in a bestselling book, pamphlets
with eery illustrations, the casual insistence
of God's eternal love, and our inescapable peril.
These are not the words we long to hear
on our front porches on autumn Saturdays,
while the neighbors burn piles of leaves.
Are we disconcerted by their tireless faith?

Honestly, we don't want what they have.
Not the path, not the knock, not the few chosen,
not the absence of holidays, not the fear
of strange, transfused blood. And still,
they visit, like relatives we attempt to lose track of,
who stop in for iced tea and an endless slide show.
We would rather hide in a hall closet, waiting,
silently praying that they will go away.

Versions of myself

I am afraid of envelopes,
the origins of their glue,
the humming mouth of their fixed seal,
the wormy lining that keeps us
from spying on their contents.

I am a girl with a note, paper
folded again and again on top of itself,
a linking pattern of letters,
eventually turned square.
I rhyme words into the shapes of things—
verbal origami—the tapered beeswax candle,
I melt and handle, the finch with one wing;
I fashion him a sling.
They drip and limp across my page.

I am the color you see in the brightest shadows
at midday. I invite you in,
cover you with my red-lined cape
and then we disappear, little by little,
as you chase me in small circles, shielding
your eyes from the glare.

I never believed the magician and his saw,
that overused tuxedo with fading lapels,
the suspicious plastic wand, poking at the air.
I've always wanted to rush the stage,
set free both sides of the girl in sequins
and rouge, boxed and halved. I would examine
that clean cut dividing her,
figure out if she'll ever be whole again.

Praying Mantis

Is there a different God for you, all green angles
and ambush? You bend your elbows and pray
in silence, disguising yourself
as a blade of September grass.
Are you asking to be a leaf?
Are you begging for forgiveness for your easy sex,
so indiscriminate on my screen door?
Or is your mercy reserved for the post-coital sin
of devouring your unwitting mate's ripe head?
And just as quickly as you drop from the door jamb
onto my shoulder, you are now a stone
on the front walk, ever blending in, always waiting,
patient in your mirror costume.
You fit in my hand.
You steal into my laundry room.
I am compelled to rescue you, lift you out
into the yard on a piece of paper.
Sometimes I shut you up in my casement window—
a temporary prison, a movie screen,
a wood-trimmed heaven.
Are you waiting for an answer?
A whispered sign across the patio, a stick
dropped from the Almighty,
that you might mimic and chew.
And who am I to say that you cannot be forgiven?
And who am I to judge your postulant posture?
Devout in what you are, true
to your insect sect, driven by instinct
simply to pray.

Keyhole

First, I imagine a keyhole, the patina
of oxidized metal, how the edges have rounded
after how many creaky-door openings, how many
clicks of the lock? What greetings
stood like the door itself—weighted, awaited—heavy
and swinging *hellos* and, of course, the slams goodbye.
This all goes back to the lock factory,
its barred windows, smelling of liquid metal,
the heat of summer, workmen in drenched thin jumpsuits
of blue cotton, all sweat and nicotine, empty Coca-Cola
bottles scattered, cloth handkerchiefs used for wiping upper lips
and foreheads. Lock molds in countless stacks,
one after another, conveyor belt of future security,
with carved patterns, like jewelry for the wrists of doorknobs,
another era of craftsmanship and art.
As men stood in the heat, staring, would they imagine
the relief of a key in the lock at the end of the day,
or pretend to look through the keyhole to the side of secrets?
A diary acted out in an upstairs bedroom, the tangle
of quiet and not quiet, one sheet
on the hardwood floor, four feet
exposed at the end of the mattress, a late breeze
against brocade curtains. We see only what we can,
limited by shape and depth, angle and purpose.
Both hands open, held flat against the door, one eye open
and the other closed, kneeling before an opening
whose only promise is to keep us out.

Sea Wasp

Poison blue, missing-breath blue, blue of bruise and deep ocean.
Tissue-paper blue, oxygen blue, blue shovel and sand bucket.
Angry blue, vein blue, plucked-petal blue, blue of morning
sky and a newborn's eyes.
Foreign blue, cerulean-oil-paint blue, the blue that is a part
of red. Gasping blue, scuba-tank blue, anemone blue,
the blue of terrycloth on tan skin. Empty black-blue, eyelid blue,
lashing-hook blue, the blue of shallow water at your feet.
The hiding blue beneath the skin, the blue of falling
and landing. Extra blue, when the blue turns beyond purple
back to blue, like late dusk, like curtains, like shipwrecks,
like endings.

Patrice de la Tour du Pin

I cannot conjugate a verb
in your language. What is the past tense
of narcissus? Is there an imperfect form of amber?
I read your poetry and believe it is more exquisite
because I have no idea what you mean.
It is the surrender to sound, an unannounced pattern of rolled Rs,
and the letter Y, when I expected the letter L.
Everything in your poem is an addictive verb
or a redolent adjective. Your fingers reek
of mint leaves; the slopes behind your knees are as white
as morning milk in back-porch glass bottles; you
are more blonde in the summer, in direct noon sunlight,
somewhere near to where there is an ocean, and a blanket
in wide blue and red stripes. The perfumes I smell,
not an essence of primrose, not vaguely floral, but closer
to something that spills from a shaker in a bakery.
Perhaps cinnamon, maybe cloves? Who knows?
My translation is so loose that it is already lost
in the wind that tugs the laundry off of your backyard clothesline.
Your words are like the patterns of clothespins on the early
     summer lawn:
familiar, repeated, and wanting to be flower stems, or grass blades,
or blue feathers that once flew.

Love writes a letter

Complicated. She writes at such a slant that the words
are nearly illegible. The entire page resembles a convoluted
doodle that might remind you of a lop-sided heart.
She is easily distracted, and her pen is filled with plum-colored ink.
The letters are too loopy, she dots each letter I, not with smiley faces,
but with stars—he guesses this is to show that she is impulsive,
reckless, edgy. He would rather she wrote in her own blood.
He would rather that this letter were a purple tattoo across
the small of her thin, pink back. Maybe spelled in Chinese symbols,
maybe written between a pair of over-sized bird wings. A foreign script
would be better, because her words only make him angry.
She is an invitation he refuses to respond to, still unopened,
fixed with a thumbprint-sized lump of blue sealing wax.
And she is always wasting words, and heavy paper. The piece
he holds now, with its edges trimmed in pressed forget-me-nots, feels
like an announcement. He will read only the first line.
He never reads past the first line. But he does keep every page
she sends, tying them with cooking twine, as if binding
a Thanksgiving bird. He has no reason to keep them, no desire
to read them all the way through, or ever again. Still, they are there,
in a red box on his closet shelf, next to a stack of old hats, on top
of some books he's been meaning to return to the library,
not so much hidden, as wanting to be forgotten.

Thirty Days

The calendar collapses on itself,
like the white squares of an igloo
at the beginning of a thaw.
Rows melt into each other
as water's cold twin turns her back, spreads
iced limbs in every direction a map's arrows know.
Thirty days, one full moon,
fall shakes hands with winter—
the familiar gesture and nod.
They have met before, under this bare aspen,
across the ridge from the last
of orange and yellow.
I age a decade each week.
My scar, a timeline extending
to everything that can't be seen below.

I turn on myself; my tectonic plates shift
and build new mountains.
This landscape is unfamiliar—
I did not pack the right gear,
my compass cracked last week,
and there is altitude sickness to contend with.
If I could just breathe.
What was for me is now against me,
like something sharp in my pocket,
with a cold handle that opens accidentally,
like an alarm sounding during deep sleep,
too soon, too loud, too close to the end of a dream,
a dream where I am me, but you don't know
it is me, but you are you,
and I know it is you.

Full Term

> For Julie and Jane Fraser

Calendar squares divide ten four-week months. Days separated by the plain shape of equal sides. You, my round cell cluster, the shape of eternity, bubbles, holes. You divide, multiply, become the square root—defy calculus, any equation, most statistics. They replace our words with numbers, turn our tongues to ticker tape. Odds. We cannot bet black or red. Lady luck has already wrapped a thigh around her own high roller. Our dice, made of lead, have edges pocked from hitting the table's sides too hard. Their dots rub off in our palms. Smooth with loss.

Living expectation. From the beginning we want you to be all of us—a pair of eyes so pale they seem clear, a purer blue than melting snow. You are the loopy swirl of a new fingerprint, every dark budding eyelash root. Matter conforms to humanity, behold shape and movement. They form your parts, dots on a screen—reduce you to flickers of shadow and light. A magic wand drags across an oiled belly. They drain us with needles. Abracadabra. They steal fluids and tissue and use them like mirrors to distract us from your miracles. Disguise your invisible mystery. Cover us with a sheet and, *voila*, make us disappear.

Strangers dare to palm this balloon, create static that shocks on contact. Ask which sex, guess the due date. Parts of you are missing. Do I tell? They may ignore the curl of ivory dominoes, lined up and collapsed, that form a spine, perfectly carved. They may fear your kicks, hiccups, any movement beneath my shirt. Some suspect the vibrations are due to explosives taped to my waist. Beautiful sticks of dynamite. A heavy wire-wound silver clock. But your pink padded heels disarm me.

Her life within me may be the whole of her life. Suddenly, my belly is a world. Our voices are constellations, our laughter—comets. Our hands rubbing my stomach are tiny tsunamis, just strong enough to turn her tides. Still, why do I feel like the astronaut? Tethered from twisted cord to orbiting ship, the umbilical acrobat. I connect with, but am apart from, the presence of your beauty, love. Suspended, I float in light reflecting off of your seas. Waiting, I count each rotation, relying on their promise of delivery.

What do you think about me being sad?

I know you think that I am just another melancholy poem,
written in a blue-painted room, at a wooden desk, by moonlight.
When the truth is, I was written outside, on a bus stop bench at noon,
while the poet ate a salted pretzel from a street vendor's cart.
Don't judge me if my cicada won't sing mournfully. It isn't up to you
to decide what I've lost (my keys) or who I am missing (my dog).
And maybe it isn't raining, the windows of this cottage are not crying.
Maybe today I am just sad without reason—because I had a dream
about a boy in a plaid shirt, because I didn't walk through the
    yellow leaves,
because it smells like wet soil and ashes outside.
But you still get to misplace your sadness onto mine. What better way
to be sad than to read a poem, this downturn of letters
that run like tears, always pointing towards the last word?

Kirsten Casey spent 20 short years producing this collection of poetry. After earning her MFA in Creative Writing from San Francisco State University, she did extensive research work in procreation, laundry, chauffeuring, and sleeplessness. A California Poet in the Schools, she lives in the Sierra Nevada foothills with her husband of 21 years, her three beautiful, loud children, and one neurotic dog. You can find Kirsten's blog at outofthelivingbody.tumblr.com.

www.ingramcontent.com/pod-product-compliance
Lightning Source LLC
Chambersburg PA
CBHW020947090426
42736CB00010B/1310